I0901448

BOCK TO BOCK

a collection of hymns and gospel songs

Arranged for

Organ and Piano Duet

by

FRED BOCK

Fred Bock Music Company would like to thank several publisher-friends who have graciously allowed their valuable copyrights to be used in this book: Fox Music Publications, Gaither Music, Inc., Hope Publishing Co., and Singspiration, Inc.

There's Something About that Name

Hammond Organs
Upper: 00 7008 004
Lower: 00 6644 440
Pedal: 54
Full Vibrato

Other Organs
Upper: Flutes 8,′ 4,′ 2′
Lower: Strings and Flutes 8,′ 4,′
Pedal: Gedeckt 16,′ Flute 8′
Full Vibrato

WILLIAM J. GAITHER
Arr. by Fred Bock

Lower
mf
mf
8va
mp
ped.

Upper
mf
8va
8va
8va
8va
10
white note thumb gliss.
3

Slower
Lower
a tempo
f
a tempo
f
8va
8va

a little slower
mp
Upper
ped.
ad lib.
L.H.
ten.
mp
Upper
mp
L.H.
p
Lower
Lower
p

Moment by Moment

Hammond Organs
Upper: 00 8882 246
Lower: 00 7055 222
Pedal: 44
Full Vibrato

Other Organs
Upper: Diapason 8,′ 4′
Strings 8,′ 4′
Lower: Flutes, light strings 8′
Pedal: Light 16,′ 8′
Full Vibrato

MAY WHITTLE MOODY
Arr. by Fred Bock

mf
f

mf
Lower
mf
f
Upper

8va
mf
ped.
f
8va-

8va
f
8va
Lower
f
mf
mp
Smoothly Upper
Lower
p
8va
p
p

Grace Greater than our Sin

Hammond Organs
Upper: 02 7876 545
Lower: 00 6655 432
Pedal: 55
Full Vibrato

Other Organs
Upper: Full Ensemble 8,′ 4,′ 2′
Lower: Strings and Flutes 8,′ 4′
Pedal: Flutes 16,′ 8′
Full Vibrato

DANIEL B. TOWNER
Arr. by Fred Bock

Smoothly

f
Lower

Upper
Upper
Lower f

8va
8va
L. H.
f

8va
f
mf
Pedal legato
mp
p
pp

And Can it Be?

Hammond Organs
Lower: 02 7868 446
Pedal: 64
Vibrato off

Other Organs
Lower: Full organ, no reeds
8,′ 4,′ 2′
Pedal: Full, 16,′ 8′
Gt. to Ped.
Vibrato off

Majestically

THOMAS CAMPBELL
Arr. by Fred Bock

✳ Second time, play both hands in octaves

8va
8va
mf
L.H.

f
f
mf
mf
mf
mf
mf
mf
mf
f

8va
ff
back to beginning
(play octaves)
1.
back to beginning
8va
2.
ff
ff

I'll Tell the World that I'm a Christian

Hammond Organs
Upper: 00 8080 700
Prepare: 32 7848 025
Lower: 01 7746 025
Pedal: 54
Full Vibrato

Other Organs
Upper: Flutes, Strings 16,′ 8,′ 4,′ 2,′ 2 ⅔
Prepare: Clarinet 8′
Lower: Full organ with Diapasons 8,′ 4,′
Pedal: Flutes 16,′ 8′ Sw. to Ped. 8′
Full Vibrato

BAYNARD FOX
Arr. by Fred Bock

smoother
L. H.
mf
smoother
mf
8va
mf
8va
ten.
f
ten.
f
ten.
ten.

8va
f
mf

mf
f
Clarinet 8′
mp
A♯ 00 8080 700(Vibrato 1)
ten.
broaden
ten.
mf
broaden
Upper
ten.
Lower
L. H.
ten.
ten.
ten.

Lower
8va
8va
as in the beginning
8va
as in the beginning

8va
mp
slower
ad lib. (lightly)
8va
pp
8va
Upper
mf
Clarinet 8′
mp
Lower
Reduce Pedal 43

Love Was When

Hammond Organs
Upper: 00 8070 600
Prepare: 55 7808 007
Lower: 00 7653 443
Pedal: 53
Full Vibrato

Other Organs
Upper: Oboe 8′
Prepare: Full Organ, Flutes, Strings, 16,′ 8,′ 4,′ 2′
Lower: Flutes and Strings and Celestes, 8,′ 4′
Pedal: Flutes 16,′ 8′
Full Vibrato

DON WYRTZEN
Arr. by Fred Bock

Full organ
registration
Lower

Change registration as
it was at the beginning
tempo as in the beginning
Upper
Lower

f
R.H.
8va
f

mf
mf
f
beginning registration
mp
pp
pp
mp
soft flute

For Bill Fasig and John Innes

Lead on, O King Eternal

Hammond Organs
Upper: 00 4704 001
Vibrato Chorus 1
Lower: 01 7848 335
Vibrato off
Pedal: 64

Other Organs
Upper: Flute and Strings 8′
Flute Celeste, String Celeste
Lower: Full Organ 8,′ 4,′ 2,′
Pedal: Flutes 16,′ 8′
Gt. to Ped.
Vibrato off

HENRY SMART
Arr. by Fred Bock

f
mf
Upper

reduce pedal
f

8va
f
ff

Near the Cross

Hammond Organs
Upper: 00 6007 000
Lower: 00 5634 333
Pedal: 53
Full Vibrato

Other Organs
Upper: Flutes 8,′ 2′
Lower: Strings 8,′ String Celeste
Flute 4′
Pedal: Flute 16′
Full Vibrato

WILLIAM DOANE
Arr. by Fred Bock

L.H.
mf
Lower
R. H.
L. H.

a little brighter
f
1- f
2- mf
mf
a little brighter
f
1- f
2- mf
Lower
mf
Light rhythm

(play 2x only)
mf
Upper
mf
ad lib.
ten.
ten.
mp
8va
pp
Lower
mp
p
pp

Healer of Broken Hearts

Hammond Organs
Upper: 00 7807 006
Lower: 00 5644 331
Pedal: 53
Full Vibrato

Other Organs
Upper: Flutes 8,′ 4,′ 2,′
Lower: Stopped Diapason 8′
Flutes 8,′ 4′
Pedal: Light Flutes 16,′ 8′
Full Vibrato

GEORGIA STIFFLER
Arr. by Fred Bock

Light tempo
mp
mf
Upper
mp
mf
Light tempo
3
L. H.
Lower

Upper
mf
f
8va

to Coda
Upper
Lower
mf
to Coda
mp
Upper
Lower

mf
Upper
8va
mf
mp
mf
CODA
rit
mp
Upper
p

For Steve Quesnel

Children of the Heavenly Father

Hammond Organs
Upper: 00 4554 444
Vibrato off
Lower: 00 5625 402
Vibrato 1
Pedal: 52

Other Organs
Upper: Strings 8,′ 4,′ 2′
Vibrato off
Lower: Strings and Flutes 8,′ 4′
String celeste, Flute celeste

SWEDISH MELODY
Arr. by Fred Bock

Gently

mf
L. H.
f
Add full vibrato
Lower
f